FAST-ATTACK SUBMARINE

The Seawolf Class

Gregory Payan

HIGH
interest
books

Children's Press
High Interest Books
A Division of Grolier Publishing
New York / London / Hong Kong / Sydney
Danbury, Connecticut

Contributing Editor: Mark Beyer
Book Design: Nelson Sa

Photo Credits: Cover © Jim Brennan/U.S. Navy; pp. 5, 6 © Corbis; p. 9 ©
Yogi, Inc./Corbis; p. 10 © Corbis; p. 12 © Yogi, Inc./Corbis; pp 16, 18, 20, 23
© Corbis; p. 25 © Robert Garvey/Corbis; p. 26, 29 © John E. Gay Cheif
Photographer/U.S. Navy; p. 31 © Yogi, Inc./Corbis; p. 32 © John E. Gay
Cheif Photographer/U.S. Navy; p. 34 © Corbis; pp. 37, 39 © U.S. Navy; p.
41 © Roger Ressmeyer/Corbis.

Visit Children's Press on the Internet at:
http://publishing.grolier.com

Library of Congress Cataloging-in-Publication Data

Payan, Gregory.
    Fast-attack submarine : the Seawolf class / by Gregory Payan.
    p. cm.—(High-tech military weapons)
    Summary: Presents a brief history of the submarine as an attack weapon
      with emphasis on the most modern Seawolf class, which includes the
      USS Seawolf, the USS Connecticut, and the USS Jimmy Carter.
    ISBN 0-516-23338-6 (lib. bdg.)—ISBN 0-516-23538-9 (pbk.)
    1. Seawolf (Submarine)—Juvenile literature. 2. Submarines (Ships)—
    Juvenile literature.
    [1. Seawolf (Submarine) 2. Submarines.] I. Title. II. Series.

VA65.S429 P39 2000
623.8'257—dc21   99-058094

CONTENTS

INTRODUCTION

The submarine once was the highlight of the U.S. Navy. More than two hundred movies have been made about submarine battle. Many books also were written about the heroic submariners who served on these ships during wartime. Today, fewer and fewer submarines are being built. This is because of the cost and time it takes to build a modern submarine. In the future, the United States plans to have a smaller fleet (group) of submarines. They will be faster, quieter, and more deadly. More than one billion dollars was spent on researching and developing the newest class (type) of submarine. The *SSN Seawolf* promises to lead the U.S. Navy in the twenty-first century.

Submarines lurk like giant whales beneath the sea.

CHAPTER 1

THE ATTACK SUBMARINE

All submarines were once attack submarines. Submarines sped beneath the sea and found enemy ships. Once the enemy was located, the sub rose close to the ocean's surface. The captain used a periscope to see above the water. The periscope allowed the captain to see the target ship. The captain ordered "Fire!" Torpedoes were launched at the enemy ship. The torpedoes hit their target and sunk the enemy ship. This is how submarines worked in World War I (1914–1918) and World War II (1939–1945).

These missile tubes hold the Tomahawk. Fast-attack submarines have a variety of weapons to use.

The first nuclear attack submarine was made in 1955. This submarine was called the *USS Nautilus*. A nuclear missile is a rocket that uses an atomic bomb to destroy its enemy. Missiles travel through the air while searching out their targets. The nuclear missile sub moves silently beneath ocean waters and waits. What is it waiting for? It is waiting for orders to get close to the surface. Once the sub is close enough, it fires its nuclear missiles. This is all a nuclear missile submarine does. It does not search for enemy ships. It does not carry and pick up troops. It does not patrol harbors. It does not lay mines. However, the attack submarine does all of these missions. The attack submarine is a much more exciting and capable high-tech weapon.

The *Seawolf* attack submarine is the smartest, fastest, and deadliest submarine ever built. How can a submarine be smart? A

The Seawolf Class submarines are packed with computers to help them listen for the enemy.

submarine gets its information from computers. These computers are operated by trained men. Using computers, men, and weapons, the *Seawolf* outsmarts its enemies.

WHY THE SEAWOLF IS SO GOOD

The *Seawolf* is loaded with powerful computers. All of these computers are linked together in one system. This system is called

the BSY-2 combat system. The BSY-2 helps the men who work on the sub to work more quickly. It helps the crew to fire torpedoes quickly and to reload the torpedo tubes. In fact, the BSY-2 controls all of the weapons and targeting systems. Targeting systems aim torpedoes and missiles at their targets. The BSY-2 makes torpedoes and missiles more accurate. The BSY-2 also helps to drive the sub and keep it going in the right direction. However, all of these systems won't do any good unless the ship carries the proper weapons.

THE BEST WEAPONS IN THE WORLD

The *Seawolf* begins any attack using torpedo launchers. These launchers are tubes that are located on both sides of the ship's front. These tubes can launch missiles and torpedoes. Missiles travel through the air. Torpedoes travel underwater.

Missiles shot from submarines are guided by electronic targeting systems.

There are three types of weapons that Seawolf Class submarines can carry. They are the Mark 48 ADCAP torpedo, the Harpoon antiship missile, and the Tomahawk cruise missile.

The MK 48 ADCAP Torpedo

A torpedo is a long bomb that looks like a big fish. It has a motor that moves it through the

water. Torpedoes used to be aimed at ships as a rifle is aimed at a target. If the aim was off, the target was missed. Modern torpedoes use computer devices that help them to find their targets. Once a torpedo finds its target, it closes in and explodes on contact.

The MK 48 ADCAP torpedoes are made to destroy two things. They are used against nuclear submarines that travel in deep water. They are also used against surface ships. The Mark 48 ADCAP was first used in 1988. The MK 48 ADCAP torpedoes are 19 feet long and weigh 3,695 pounds. They can travel more than 5 miles. This is their range. They can be used at more than 1,200 feet underwater. They travel more than 28 knots per hour (32.2 mph). These torpedoes can use active and passive sonar. They can be used with or without wire guidance. Also, if the torpedo misses its target, it can turn around and go after it again.

The Mark 48 ADCAP torpedo is the most high-tech torpedo used by any country in the world.

Homing Torpedoes and Wire Guidance Torpedoes

Active homing torpedoes send out sonar signals while searching for the target. Sonar is an electronic device. It sends out sound

What's a Knot?

A knot is a unit of measure. A knot measures the speed of something traveling in water. One knot is equal to 1.15 miles per hour. A ship traveling at 10 knots is moving at 11.5 miles per hour.

waves that pass through the water. If the sound waves hit something, they bounce off the object and come back to the torpedo. These sonar waves tell the torpedo where the target is. Once found, the torpedo follows the target.

Passive homing torpedoes listen for noise made by a target. This noise is usually the engine of the target ship. Once the noise is "heard" by the torpedo, it follows its target.

Wire guidance torpedoes are launched like regular torpedoes. However, there is a copper wire connected from the torpedo back to the ship. Think of the wire as a spool of thread. The spool unrolls as the torpedo shoots toward its target. This copper wire is used by the crew to send messages to the torpedo. These messages guide the torpedo to its target. There is a reason the torpedo uses a wire rather than a radio signal. You see, torpedoes are pretty slow. Many ships can outrun torpedoes if they hear them coming. When a torpedo uses its sonar, a ship is able to hear it by using its own sonar. Using the wire lets the crew steer the torpedo toward its target without using sonar. Now the enemy ship can't hear the torpedo. Only when the torpedo is

500 feet from the ship does its sonar turn on.
Now the torpedo homes in on the ship before
it can turn or get away.

The Harpoon Missile

The Harpoon missile is a rocket that carries a
bomb. The Harpoon missile is launched from
the torpedo tube inside the submarine. Once
fired, it shoots out of the water and flies

above the surface of the ocean until it reaches its target. This missile uses electronic signals to tell it where the target is. These electronic signals are called radar (RAdio Detecting and Ranging). Harpoon missiles are 15 feet long. They weigh 1,400 pounds. They travel faster than the speed of sound(545 mph). Harpoon missiles are most accurate when used on targets up to 60 miles away.

The Tomahawk Cruise Missile

The Tomahawk cruise missile is used against targets on land. It flies very close to the ground at 550 miles per hour. Tomahawk missiles are used against targets that are far away. They can fly distances of up to 1,000 miles.

The Tomahawk was first used in 1991 during the Persian Gulf War. Tomahawk cruise missiles are popular for two reasons. For one,

Harpoon missiles are used against land and sea targets.

Fast-attack submarines use the Tomahawk cruise
missile to hit targets more than 1,000 miles away.

they are very good at hitting their targets.
Also, they do not need a pilot to fly them to
their targets. Accuracy and no risk of pilot
death make the Tomahawk missile a valuable
weapon.

Mines

A mine is a bomb that floats on or below the
surface of the water. Mines explode when

something hits them. When a ship runs into a mine, the bomb explodes. This explosion puts a hole in the ship and causes it to sink. Mines are used near enemy harbors or where ships are known to travel.

Packed with Power

The *Seawolf* can carry fifty-two different missiles or torpedoes. It also can carry one hundred mines. This is called its payload. This payload is 30 percent more than any other submarine can carry. With all of these weapons, the *Seawolf* can stay near a battle longer and shoot more.

Any Seawolf Class submarine can reach 75 percent of the land on Earth for attack missions. Only 25 percent of the Earth's land is too far away for them to attack from coastal waters. However, the best weapon of all is the sub itself. It is faster and quieter than any other sub made today.

CHAPTER 2

THE HISTORY OF THE SUBMARINE

THE FIRST SUBMARINE

In 1895, John Holland built the first submarine. He named the sub the *Plunger*. The U.S. Navy paid him to build this sub. It was supposed to be the first submarine to serve in the Navy. However, Holland became worried about all of the different things that the Navy wanted the *Plunger* to do. He continued working on the *Plunger*. However, he began to build another submarine with his own money. His worries proved correct. The *Plunger* failed its tests, called sea trials.

The *USS Nautilus* was the first nuclear-powered submarine. It was launched in 1955.

Luckily, Holland had his other submarine. On April 11, 1900, the United States purchased the *Holland VI* for $160,000. It was commissioned (put into use) October 12, 1900. It was named the *USS Holland* (SS-1). The *USS Holland* had a crew of one officer and five men. Its top speed was less than 10 miles per hour. The sub used a gasoline-powered engine. While above water, the engine charged its batteries. These batteries were used to power the sub when underwater.

SUBMARINES USED IN WAR

As the years passed, a lot of time and money were used to build newer and better subs. By the end of World War I, submarines were larger and faster than Holland's first sub. Also, these new subs had better weapons. Torpedoes were faster and deadlier.

During World War II, U.S. Navy subs helped to win the war against Japan. U.S.

World War II (1939-1945) submarines used
periscopes to aim their torpedoes at enemy ships.

submarines sank 1,113 Japanese ships. Two-hundred fourteen of these ships were warships. The rest were merchant ships that carried supplies for Japan's armies. Without supplies such as bullets and guns, the Japanese could no longer fight. Of all the ships Japan lost, U.S. submarines sank more than half of them. This fact is impressive because less than two out of every one hundred U.S. Navy ships were submarines. Yet subs were responsible for more than 50 percent of the Japanese ship losses.

SUBS GO NUCLEAR

Nuclear-powered submarines were developed in 1955. There was a great need to have subs stay underwater for a long time. Enemy defenses counted on a sub's need to surface for refueling. Staying underwater for long periods of time was vital. This could be done by using nuclear power.

Nuclear-powered submarines use less energy than do gasoline-powered subs. They also make a lot less noise. They can travel up to 400,000 miles without needing to resurface. That's nearly sixteen times around the Earth! A

The nuclear reactor in a submarine works by using heat. The nuclear reactor is what holds the radioactive material. Uranium is a kind of radioactive material. The heat from the radioactive material boils water. This boiling water gives off steam. The steam turns fans that make electricity. The electricity is used to power the submarine.

A nuclear submarine only needs to
resurface to restock its food supplies.

nuclear sub only needs to resurface to restock
its food supplies. The first nuclear-powered
submarine to serve in the Navy was the *USS
Nautilus.* It was commissioned in January 1955.

THE SEAWOLF CLASS

The first Seawolf Class submarine was commissioned in 1997. A class of submarine is
judged by what it can do and how it can be
used. There are three submarines in the
Seawolf Class. The first is the *USS Seawolf*
(SSN 21). The second is the *USS Connecticut*

(SSN 22). The third is the *USS Jimmy Carter* (SSN 23). All three subs are based in Groton, Connecticut. The *Seawolf* has the number SSN 21 to show that it's an attack submarine for the twenty-first century. Both the *USS Seawolf* and the *USS Connecticut* are used by the Navy. They prowl the oceans as you read this. However, the *USS Jimmy Carter* is still under construction. It will not be in service for a few more years.

CHAPTER 3

THE HIGH-TECH SEAWOLF SUB

The *SSN Seawolf* (SSN 21) is 353 feet long and 40 feet wide. That is longer than a football field. Its width is called its beam. The beam is the boat's widest point. The *Seawolf*'s beam is seven feet wider than Los Angeles Class subs. The Los Angeles Class submarines were made before the Seawolf Class. This shape helps the *Seawolf* travel faster underwater. The *Seawolf* can hold a crew of 134 people.

Many of the details about the *Seawolf* are secret, such as how the sub was made. More importantly, the military capabilities of the

The crew prepares a Seawolf Class sub for duty.

Seawolf are secret. However, some things about the *Seawolf* are known. Its top speed is more than 35 knots per hour. Some people say the *Seawolf* can move much faster. There is a joke in the Navy. It says that *Seawolf* Captain Dave McCall can get speeding tickets at sea. Even moving at 25 knots per hour, the *Seawolf* is very quiet. It is so quiet, in fact, that it makes less noise than any other submarine does while sitting at the pier.

HEAVY METAL?

The *Seawolf* is made of metal that can bend. This metal is flexible. Most steel is brittle, which means it can crack. Steel becomes even more brittle when sitting in cold seawater deep in the ocean. The flexible steel that the *Seawolf* is made of is called high-tensile steel. This steel allows the *Seawolf*'s body, called a hull, to shrink and grow without cracking. Without flexibility, a submarine's

The metal used on each Seawolf sub is flexible to withstand deep sea pressure.

hull cannot withstand deep ocean depths. Why is this important? Because the further a sub goes beneath the ocean, the more pressure it has on its hull. Have you ever swum to the bottom of a swimming pool? As you go further down you can feel your head tighten. It feels as if someone has put you in a headlock. This is how pressure works. It's as if something is squeezing an object. Think about squeezing a tennis ball. You are placing pressure on the ball. Underwater, pressure increases at greater depths. At a depth of 2,000 feet, an automobile would be crushed.

The Navy claims that the *Seawolf* can move at depths of more than 800 feet. Experts say the sub can go down much

further. How does 2,000 feet sound? The only way the *Seawolf* can survive at this depth is because of its high-tensile steel hull.

HEARING AIDS

Sonar is one of the most important electronic tools used on a submarine. At the front of the *Seawolf* is a dome that holds the sonar equipment. As you have already learned, sonar transmits sound waves to find things underwater. The sound waves bounce off any object in the distance, back to the submarine. However, it takes time for the waves to go out and return. The total amount of time between when the waves are sent and when the waves return tells the crew how far away the object is from the sub.

WHERE THE CREW WORKS AND LIVES

Behind the sonar and torpedo rooms you will find the command and control center. This is

Submarine bunk rooms are cramped, leaving little personal space for the crew.

where the crew steers the *Seawolf*. It is where the crew uses computers to search the waters for enemies. This room is also where military decisions are made. The captain gives orders and receives reports from this room. The command and control center is the heart of the *Seawolf*.

Below the command and control center are the crew's quarters and the mess hall. These areas are cramped. They are similar in size to a small home basement with a low ceiling. The crew sleeps in beds that are stacked four-high. These beds are on either side of the room. They are separated by an aisle as wide as the one you might find on a train car. This is more cramped than the officers' quarters. Officers sleep three to a room. These rooms are a little larger than a walk-in closet. The officers spend much of their off-duty time in the wardroom. This is also where they eat. The captain is the only man onboard with a room to himself.

This narrow passage leads to the bridge.

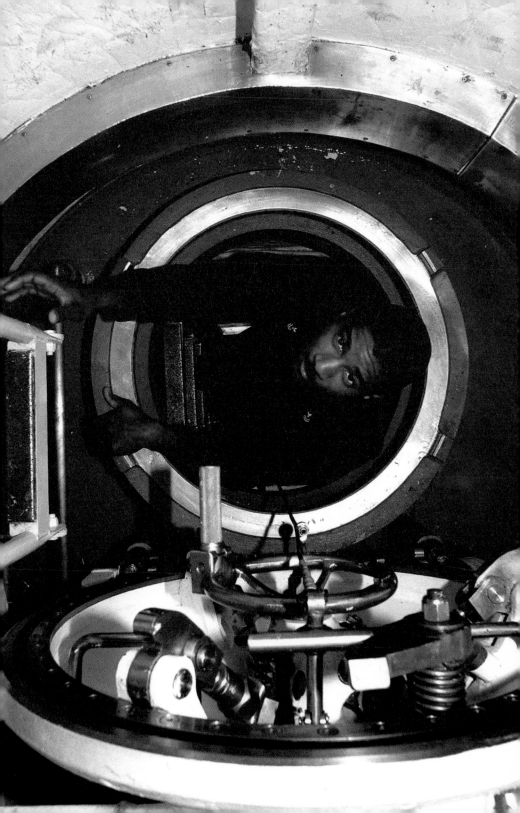

CHAPTER 4

SUBMARINE DUTIES OF TODAY AND TOMORROW

The cold war era (1946–1989) was a time of political struggle between the United States and the Soviet Union. The United States stood for democracy. The Soviet Union stood for communism. Both countries built up their military power by building weapons. These weapons included tanks, planes, and ships. The U.S. submarine force had four hundred ships during this time. However, the Soviet Union broke apart in 1989. Since then, the U.S. submarine force has shrunk. The U.S. sub force will probably never again reach four hundred ships. This is because the

Nuclear subs can navigate below the polar ice caps and surface through the ice.

United States doesn't have an enemy as powerful as was the Soviet Union. This means that four hundred subs are no longer needed.

ATTACK SUBS IN TODAY'S WORLD

The *Seawolf* is one of the last war machines made during the cold war. Experts say that only 45–55 attack submarines will be in service by the year 2000. The Seawolf Class submarines will be the most valuable members of the naval fleet. Seawolf Class submarines are able to do things that no other submarine can do. The Seawolf Class subs are able to operate under Arctic ice. Their navigation systems allow safer steering under ice. Seawolf Class subs also can break through the ice. They can move in shallow water, as well.

The Seawolf Class submarines are the fastest subs ever made. They can get to hostile ocean areas quickly. These areas are just

The construction of a Seawolf Class sub is completed in stages.

off the coasts of nations at war. Seawolf Class subs are given missions to clear the way for military strikes by other forces. Their sneaki-ness and firepower make them perfect for these missions. The *Seawolf* can destroy enemy submarines. They can attack ships. They also can attack targets on land. These are the Seawolf subs' main duties.

Seawolf Class subs have many other duties. They mine harbors and coastal areas. They spy on the enemy. Seawolf subs can get close to shallow coastal waters. Here they can send out spy forces. Later they can return and pick up these forces.

Subs must be able to land, recover, and provide supplies to Special Forces groups such as Navy SEALs. This job is very important to U.S. forces. Seawolf Class submarines do these things better than any other sub. Their ability to travel silently and attack swiftly makes them perfect for this job.

SUBMARINES FOR THE FUTURE

The third boat in the Seawolf Class is the *USS Jimmy Carter* (SSN 23). This sub will be ready for use in a few years. The Navy is making this Seawolf Class sub the best of the three.

The *Jimmy Carter* will be built with better weapons and computers for naval special warfare. The public doesn't know what these weapons are. Neither does the enemy. Once modified, this Seawolf Class sub will have a torpedo room that can be used to hold fifty soldiers. With this ability, the sub can better sneak up on the enemy. The extra soldiers

Seawolf Class submarines are commissioned in Groton, Connecticut.

will be a surprise to the enemy. The U.S. military has ordered that all future submarines be built to hold more people.

For almost one hundred years, submarines have been important to the U.S. Navy. The Seawolf Class submarine has an even more important job in today's military. Submarines on patrol today will be led for a long time by the Seawolf Class. However, a new class of submarine is being built for the future. These subs are the Virginia Class. They will not be ready for active service until 2004. For now, the Seawolf Class submarines remain one of the true high-tech weapons.

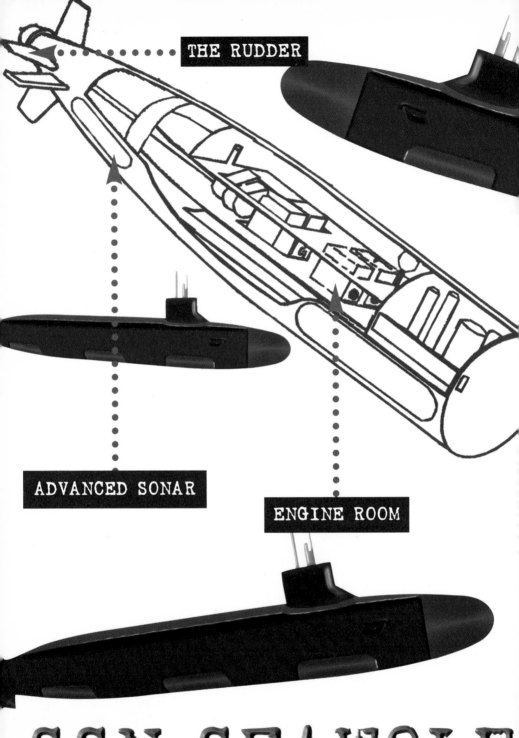

THE RUDDER

ADVANCED SONAR

ENGINE ROOM

SSN SEAWOLF

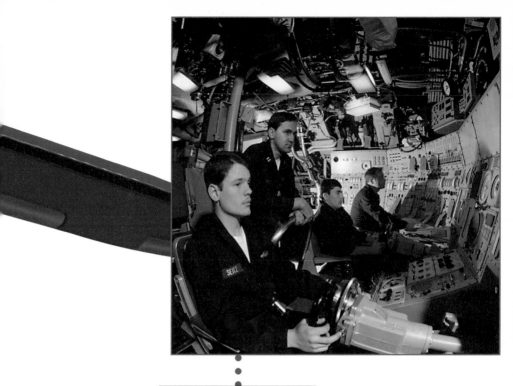

CONTROL ROOM

THE BRIDGE

TORPEDO ROOM

SONAR SPHERE

NEW WORDS

class a type of something

coastal waters ocean areas near land

cold war a time of political struggle between the United States and the Soviet Union, 1946–1989

commission to put into active service; make ready for use

fleet a group of ships

flexible capable of being bent

homing the process by which a weapon locates its target

harpoon missile a rocket that carries a bomb and is launched from the torpedo tube of a submarine

hull the body of a ship

knot one nautical mile; 6,076 feet (1,852 m)

mine a bomb that floats on or below the surface of the water, and that explodes when something hits it

payload the amount of cargo or weapons a sub can carry

periscope a tube with a lens and mirrors that lets crew members see above the water surface

radar (RAdio Detecting And Ranging) a device that sends radio waves that reflect off objects back onto a display screen; used to see objects that are far away

SEAL (SEa Air and Land) Navy special warfare person used for secret missions

sonar (SOund NAvigation Ranging) an electronic device that sends out sound waves that reflect off objects back onto a display screen; used to see objects that are underwater

submariner a person who serves on a submarine

torpedo a bomb that travels underwater and explodes when it hits something

uranium a radioactive material

wardroom the living area inside a ship

FOR FURTHER READING

Genat, Robert and Robin Genat. *Modern U.S. Navy Submarines.* Osceola,WI: Motorbooks International, 1997.

Gibbons, Tony. *Submarines.* Minneapolis, MN: The Lerner Publishing Group, 1987.

Graham, Ian. *Boats, Ships, Submarines, and Other Floating Machines.* New York: Larousse Kingfisher Chambers, Incorporated, 1993.

Sharpe, Richard. *Jane's Fighting Ships: 1998-1999.* Alexandria, VA: Jane's Information Group, 1998.

Weiss, Harvey. *Submarines and Other Underwater Craft.* New York: HarperCollins Children's Books, 1990.

RESOURCES

The Navy Office of Information

Navy Office of Information – East
805 Third Avenue, 9th Floor
New York, NY 10022-7513
(212) 784-0131

Navy Office of Information – Midwest
55 East Monroe Street, Suite 1402
Chicago, IL 60603-5705
(312) 606-0360

Navy Office of Information – Southwest
1114 Commerce Street, Suite 811
Dallas, TX 75242
(214) 767-2553

Navy Office of Information – West
10880 Wilshire Boulevard, Suite 1220
Los Angeles, CA 90035
(310) 235-7481

RESOURCES

Web Sites

Naval Technology – SSN Seawolf Class–Attack Submarine

www.naval-technology.com/index.html

This site contains information on different types of naval technology, including the SSN Seawolf Class.

USS Seawolf (SSN 575)

www.seawolf-ssn575.com

This site has information on the history of the Seawolf. It also includes links to other related sites.

INDEX

INDEX

About the Author

Gregory Payan is a freelance writer living in Queens, New York.